The Meaning, Beauty & Mystery of Dreams: Seven Guidelines and Seven Tools for Listening

Michael A. Susko

AllrOneof Us Publishing
Baltimore, Md & Huntsville, Al

THE MEANING, BEAUTY & MYSTERY OF DREAMS: SEVEN GUIDELINES AND SEVEN TOOLS FOR LISTENING

First edition. November 15, 2022.

Copyright © 2022 Michael A. Susko.

ISBN: 979-8215939499

Written by Michael A. Susko.

Table of Contents

To those who seek meaning and beauty in their dreams.

INTRODUCTION

If you were to discover a source for individualized messages that would give you a clue of what to do this day, or provide a direction that will help you fulfill your life, you would want to know more about that source. It would be like finding a treasure chest of money, one that can help fulfill your wishes. The treasures I am referring, and which can come on any night, are *dreams*.

Amazingly, we harbor within us a source which creates stories and symbols, and which attempts to personally communicate to us. The value of dreams is well known to indigenous cultures and to sacred traditions across the world. The Hebraic and Christian scriptures are filled with references to dreams messages. The story of Western civilization is littered with stories of inventors who conceived of critical ideas from their dreams. Psychological schools, such as Jungians, feature the value of dreams to a person's actualization. Given all this, why has listening and interpreting dreams become a lost art? Most schoolchildren are not taught about dreams unless their parent takes a particular interest. They will learn, as my son does, about adverbial clauses, algebraic formulae, or the reactive capacities of the alkali metal group on the periodic table. But what of the inner world and its messaging to us?

This work provides a useful guide to handle this creative, symbolic world. It is not overly complex or difficult. However, it requires attention, effort, and a willingness to deal with something we may not understand at first and may be difficult to face. But the reward is high if we can discover the utility of this "treasure box of dreams" that is yours to claim.

This work highlights the word *Listening*, rather than *Interpreting*. While we hope to gain a robust capacity to interpret dreams, the most important step is simply to listen to them. Much of our needed work is accomplished by taking this first step. We will go on now to elaborate on specific guidelines and tools, all of which have the goal of listening to dreams.

PART I
SEVEN GUIDELINES TO DREAMS

1. Listening to Your Dreams

The first rule of anything is to *listen*. In the great biblical command to love the Universal Source and your neighbor as yourself, the first word is to *Listen*. If we do not listen, any words of wisdom or messaging to us are lost and discarded. To listen, we must deem something as important or vital to us. I cannot make this happen. Rather, it an intuition or experience within us, which we sense, awakens us to say, "I need to pay attention to this," and "this is important to my life."

There may be contrary messages telling us not to pay attention, to not believe that messages from the silence of the night are important. Our society often devalues attention to the inner world, which may challenge its materialistic emphasis. Often, we are directed by cliches, like "Dreams are crazy," or they are a mixed-up hashing of your previous day. But, if we have paid attention, we know that dreams are much more. The detail, the complexity, the felt urgency, and beauty of a given dream are witness enough that we are dealing with something far beyond the cursory.

Perhaps you say you do not dream or remember your dreams. This too may be a product of cultural disregard, that faint summons found in dreams are discarded at their first entrance into our consciousness. However, if you desire to remember your dreams and take steps that show your willingness, I would wager that you will start being gifted with dreams. Perhaps simply a journal titled *My Dreams* by your bedside, where you write your first thoughts, will open the door.

The attitude of listening is perhaps brushed off and not emphasized in our culture, where doing and aggressive action are given preeminence. But if we can root our action in the deep wells of our being, I believe we are likely to have greater, ultimate success. That takes a degree of faith. It might even seem we are going far from the action we want to take. But it is a mystery in the universe, how in searching or reaching far, we come to the center, offering the solution to what we're trying to achieve.

We note here that the guidelines and tools offered are what will help us listen to our dreams. They have been gleaned from the author's own work and from other psychologists. There are several valuable books on the topic, but the one with the most influence on me is Anne Faraday's *The Dream Game.*

So, come along this journey, in which you are invited to listen to your dreams. If you do so, you will be further along the path of actualization, which grants us a full life.

2. Becoming Comfortable with Symbolic Language

Dreams mostly employ a symbolic language. We may be used to typically having and using a singular view of reality, with one concrete meaning to things. But symbols invite us to a more open-ended, polyvalent array of meanings. Symbols are an indirect communication. For example, with something painful in your life you are avoiding, the dream may represent that pain as a symbol. This visual image refracts or presents the pain in a more manageable or approachable form. In a classic example, the *Fisher King* movie has the protagonist deal with the pain of the sudden death of his wife in a car accident by becoming a knight in a medieval world of symbols. Dreams are not that extreme, but the concept is similar. The mind has an alternative language or way of communicating. It is important to be aware of this mode, least your symbolic world becomes manipulated by propagandist or advertisers who use the power of symbols to direct you.

Becoming familiar with the symbolic world may involve writing down your dreams regularly, even without interpreting them. It may involve reading symbolic literary works or studying psychologists who explore the symbolic world. But we have firsthand access to personalized symbols which are messaging us. Thus, the most direct and perhaps quickest way to understand that language is to work with your own dreams.

Interpreting symbols reminds me of looking at stars with different colors. If you look at the star directly, you perceive only the bright whiteness. If you look to the side of the star, however, you can pick up its color, such as blue. You must be relaxed and open to the symbol to interpret it and carry the meaning further. It is a gift that is also developed by practice. You will sense a resonance when you find a connection between the symbol and your life. It will be an *aha* moment when you say, "That's it!"

Why did a symbolic language or capacity develop in humans? I think it was evolutionarily useful, for our potential awareness is quite expansive and the symbolic world allows us to reach out to new frontiers. Symbols press this edge by giving us awareness beyond what we know and what we are comfortable with. In this view, the symbolic world developed to convey to us difficult and also fabulous truths, which we resist due to an inherent conservative attitude. Symbols are the playground of artists who venture into the future, but they are also integral to understanding the world from a scientific point of view.

Perhaps it is time to give an example of a symbol. I have dreamt of a human torso, which may be mine, with a bright design or geometric pattern within it. This archetypal example of a symbol could represent the soul force within us, or the essence of our being. Another description might be our center.

The symbol calls attention that a soul force or essence can be visualized and operative within us. It is something we are not constantly aware of and may even dismiss as fanciful. However, awareness of this dimension within us may prove useful in summoning our will to act, to preserving during hard times, and to centering our being as needed.

When ordinary ways of convincing us to act or change do not work, the power of symbols may have the power to move us. Symbols access a more complete dimension of ourselves, not just our thoughts or a superego telling us what we ought to do. Symbols touch upon our emotional and spiritual being and when rightly fitted for us

Thus, the dream world focuses us on the deeper truths and feelings within us. It is a gift we should not casually dismiss. It can save our lives with a warning dream, and could even save our souls, if we take to heart and listen to its message.

3. Symbols as Metaphors for a Life Situation

Perhaps the most basic approach to understanding your dreams is that they are metaphors for a life situation. In an example I like to use, if you find yourself stuck in the mud in a dream, you might ask what situation you are feeling stuck. Perhaps there is a clue from the dream setting, such as a university. You might surmise you are feeling intellectually stagnant and would benefit from taking a course in something of interest.

In a way this guideline is easy to grasp. Yet there are blind spots in our range of self-awareness, and the dream may be calling attention to a blind spot. There is a preliminary step in that you make associations to your dream imagery and see what comes to mind. This can be called "daily associations," which we will address under tools of dream interpretation.

Sometimes dreams are more archetypal and general, dealing with your entire life situation and at a time of major decision. These dreams have more force and power and lucid imagery. The more run-of-the mill dream typically addresses a more immediate situation, which is an ongoing part of your life.

Let me give an example of a metaphor for a situation, using a personal example. I'm aware that in relating dreams, we reveal more about ourselves than we suspect. But dreams are the stuff of this book, and in order to share my awareness and knowledge, I accept the price of this vulnerability.

I will take a recent dream, which has not been examined in detail, and see what metaphorical associations I can make. The first one I come across, dated 7/29/22, is rather lengthy and detailed. Let this not deter us and see if we can capture some of its meaning.

> In my dream, I am trying to get home, and I get upset that no one will accompany me through a dangerous neighborhood. I'm angry and yelling, and I shame two or three to join me.

We go through east Baltimore between Fellspoint and downtown and work our way uptown.

I stop inside a workshop of sorts. I have to turn in my work slip, an old statement of hours which has overtime for a weekend. A person at this place suggests I turn this slip in at the main office location, and he makes reference to a person watching there. I go over and talk to that person, kidding around. He becomes interested in my case and wants to carefully go over it. I wonder if that is the best resolution.

I leave, going outside, but this has taken so much time that my companions have left me, and I am on my own. I come to a crossing of sorts, step in and realize it is a canal. I'm flailing in water, and I wonder what will happen to my electronics. It's narrow though, and I have enough momentum to reach the other side and grab onto some bars. I barely pull myself up. I check my phone and the power light still shows. I suppose I will arrive, but it will be late.

This dream has different elements, but at its essence, it is about my journeying "home" and the persons traveling with me. It turns out I lose my immediate companions because of a business, bureaucratic delay. Next, I come into a more symbolic situation, crossing a canal that is dangerous. But the canal is narrow, and I'm able to manage due to my prior momentum.

This dream uses both ordinary situations such as walking through a neighborhood, with a more obvious symbolic reality such as crossing a canal. The canal is suggesting to me that I may face barriers, but there is reason to hope. The canal is narrow enough, and there are bars to grasp at the other end. And in the dream, I surface with my phone's power light still on. True, I'll be late for whatever, but I have survived.

What is the life situation here? I think it has partly to do with the reality of the Covid for the past two or three years. Our relationships have struggled, especially with small groups. There is also the suggestion that racial attitudes about "dangerous neighborhoods" as well as business or economic matters can interfere with our relationships. So, I would say that the dream broadly relates to the struggle, given all the medical, economic and political uncertainty, as we attempt to make a re-entry with companions into society. At least, this is what I come with for now.

We can see there can be much texture and subtlety to a longer dream. But the challenge presented here is to find how a given dream relates to our life. Particularly, we want to understand the symbolic resonance of the dream's images, which may harbor more intensity, and which is our deep self speaking to us.

4. Dreams are Often About Relationships

One valuable insight from Ann Faraday's *The Dream Game* is that dreams are often about relationships. Someone would appear in your dream and feelings about the person would emerge. Often, the dream was an indicator to get in touch with that person.

I have a friend and former colleague from Baltimore for decades, who had unexpectedly dropped off from having contact without a specific reason. I wrote to him after his wife died about a year ago, and he wrote back saying "yours," in the reply, which gave me heart. I feel like I should get in touch with him in a significant way, yet I am hesitant. My hurt is such that I fear getting back in touch, least I be hurt more. He has appeared in recent dreams where the dynamics of the relationship are at play. Here is one dated on a Sunday, May 29, 2022.

> In my dream, I am at my friend's house who is having a meal with his spouse and others. I don't join them at the table due to Covid. My brother John is there too. There is a back room, which is my childhood room, with plants by a window. There is also an aquarium which is nearly empty of water, and I drain it some more. It's more finished in terms of being cleaned out. But I don't actually complete the job and leave some inner parts toppled over.

> In a second part, I share with my friend about my dreams and the meaning of the dreams, and become emotional. There is a barrier between us, and when I look around, it seems he is laying down, absorbed in something else. I ask him if he heard what I was saying, and he responds, "I don't care."

In this case there are a lot of deep dynamics at play. This couple were like second parents to me, so I am not surprised to find my brother John in the house, nor my childhood room. Even though I am at my friend's house, I am no longer at the table. In my childhood room, there is a plant, a sign of hope, but the aquarium, usually filled with life, is almost "finished."

The dream's second part imagines an encounter where I reveal my dreams and my deep emotional tie to my friend. But the response the dream shows me, is that the person does not want contact, nor does he care. We note here that dreams do not sugar coat reality, but will directly express its perceived truth.

Looking back now, I wonder if this dream is suggesting that I don't initiate contact in the sense of attempting a deep emotional outreach, as my friend has moved on. Usually, the expectation is that a dream will encourage to get back in touch with persons we have neglected. In this case, the message appears different and more difficult. I can't say this particular relationship is resolved, and I don't know how things will end. But we may wrestle in our dreams, as in our life, with our relationships.

When I woke up this morning, I tried to remember my dream, but failed. I had this thought, however, about the deep roots of dreams from our past and their projection into the future. Dreams come from deep emotional roots within us, back to the marsupials who are the first mammal-like creatures to have REM sleep, an indicator of dreaming. The mammalian legacy granted us deep emotional bonds between child and parent, which extended evolutionarily to broader social links with primates. Dreams are also rooted in spirituality and questions of the future, which is not yet. Thus, dreams involve a deep resonance with our evolutionary being, and also our future and our spiritual becoming. How our future bonds emerge and develop are intense concerns of our dream being.

5. Archetypal Dreams at Significant Life Junctures

A dream can take on a more general significance, such as showing the broad stages of your life, past and potential future. These dreams have a more dramatic and enigmatic quality to them and feel as if they have special importance. We might consider them more direct messages from our deep self or the spiritual realm. This is best illustrated by a dream I had while I was in college in my early twenties, the time when one is establishing a personal vision of the universe. I was at a Catholic college in the deep south, and I had a study room on an upper floor of a monastery. Eventually, I started sleeping there and, once discovered, the abbot allowed me to stay.

I go by memory now, as I am at a coffee shop and don't have my files with me. The dream had four stages and I remember easily the last two. Then the other two stages come back to me, as this imagery must be deeply embedded within me. The dream starts by me viewing the faint impressions of a green snake in the grass. Is it one or two? Then it emerges as a rattlesnake in plain view with a dark checkerboard pattern. In the third stage, the snake stops by a wall and turns into a fat yellow snake with large black blotches. Last, the snake grows legs under it and changes into a translucent white horse. The horse rises and attacks me.

At the time I interpreted this dream as stages in my life. It starts with consciousness being in an incipient form, like the nearly visible snake in the grass. Are we one with the "mother" or are we a separate being is the question raised as we emerge out of the "matrix." In our early childhood, we are largely invisible to ourself, coming in and out of view, and our remembrance of events is only a fraction and selective. The second stage is a more developed one and is in plain sight. The snake has a clear checkerboard pattern rather than being unicolor, so it is more complex. This stage represented coming into consciousness, like the period of adolescence. The rattlesnake identification may symbolize danger, when youth experiments with limits. The next stage is more colorful and dramatic in appearance, with a stark contrast in color. It suggests that opposites are more pronounced now. The snake also becomes still as it is stopped by a wall. It represents a period of apparent inactivity and absorption in inner processes. This was a critical stage for I related it at the time to a dramatic past experience. It could be considered a breakdown experience, a spiritual emergence experience, or what I called a *symbolic experience.* I dropped out of college and became immersed in a symbolic world where I was unable to function in a normal way. This dream was telling me that this too was part of my life stages, that it should be affirmed and integrated. Thus, the snakes represented stages of my life, in which the self becomes more fully conscious and actualized.

The last stage of the dream was unexpected and the most difficult to interpret. The animal changed from a legless snake to the much larger horse, and its color became an intense white. The translucent horse represents a spirit consciousness with more dynamic movement. However, the horse attacked me and that was unsettling. I wondered if the horse attacking me represented a struggle between the spiritual and the bodily dimension. Often dreams are not fully interpretable immediately and leave a loose end or something hanging. This was a rather large loose end, however. Looking back, I see the dream portended the future, an ongoing struggle between body and spirit, which I had not fully integrated. Now I might imagine that this spirit horse has become tamed and that I can ride the current energy it provides to do good.

In my college years, I created a mandala pattern based on this dream, which divided the phenomenon of the world into these four stages. It included, not only our life stages but angles, colors, and a broad range of associations such as the butterfly moving from an egg, to caterpillar, to chrysalis, and on to the Imago or butterfly. I edited a literary journal, entitled *Imago*, which divided the works into those four categories.

We may not all be gifted with remembering our archetypal dreams. Yet I would invite you to be open to receiving them, and if one occurs, not to casually dismiss it as crazy stuff. Often there is a dragon at the gate in dreams. It's a strong image that causes you to remember the dream, but also might deter you from reflecting on the dream and its meaning. Here, being attacked by the translucent horse may have deterred me. It takes some courage to listen and find meaning in our dreams. For one, you risk facing the fierceness of your being, as represented by the archetypal world. This wildness and fierceness are present in all of us. Ideally, it should be recognized and channeled into doing the good. The unwitting following of another's wildness, who may have manipulated this archetypal world for selfish ends, is a source of much evil in the world. Our antidote is to become fully conscious of these dimensions in ourselves and integrate them successfully into our being. When properly integrated, we choose to do the most good for ourselves and others, following the great commands of the world religions.

6. Dreams Often Deal with Shadow Energy

There is a shadow side of our being which we avoid recognizing. It could deal with murderous impulses or sexual feelings, for example. The pioneering psychologist Carl Jung asked us to integrate our shadow side, suggesting we could find hidden gold there. Likewise, a contemporary such as Al Galves has written a book called *Harnessing Your Dark Side: Mastering Jealousy, Rage, Frustration and Other Negative Emotions*. For myself, I found that when I do a letter about my day, the frustrations and negative things are often an important teacher and an important part of the fabric that weaves the day.

As our conscious mind writes off certain areas as negative, they may appear in our dreams for consideration. These troublesome images or situations may be like the dragon of the gate, already mentioned in the archetypal section, which keeps us from reflecting upon the dream further. Here is a recent dream, dated 8/15/22, where I find myself in prison, not a flattering place to be.

> In my dream I am in a prison. For some reason I have been put on harsher restriction so that I have less freedom. A youngish woman with dark hair is in control, who does not bend her will. There is still, however, a modicum of freedom for me. I wonder what I will eat. There are meals out for us that are catered, and I'm surprised at this extravagance. For some reason I have permission to leave the grounds, but I must come back on my own. I am running back and am surprised how well I can run, and how lazy I have been before. The realization of being in a prison has energized me.

The dream presents an awareness that I am in prison along with an uncertainty and variability in freedom I have. On one hand I am constrained against my will, but on the other hand, I have freedom to leave for periods. This awareness of how I handle my freedom, in contrast to being in prison, has energized me.

This occasionally recurring dream for me raises the question: In what way or in what situation am I being restrained, being kept from expressing my freedom? It also leads to the question as to the identity of the dark-haired woman. Is she an avatar of my mother who was overly strict, which I then project upon my wife?

Interestingly, the limitations of prison are contrasted with accepting the blessings and freedoms that are also present. Having contrasts like these are part of the structures of dreams, which we will elaborate more on later.

Related to prison imagery are dreams in which we have committed a terrible crime, such as a murder. In the dream we can feel the weight of that and how it would be such a great burden to carry through life. What is the meaning or value of such a dream? My son suggested it got you to feel what it would be like to have done such an act. I concurred it would create a unique empathy. Another possibility is that the "murder" is more symbolic, that it is about hate and how we might cut out persons or ghost them from our lives. I don't have a clear answer for why such things appear in the dream. But a partial answer has been suggested to me lately. When horrible acts are done by persons in our society, we assume the individual is solely responsible. We, however, ask: how have I participated or allowed such acts? In any good or bad thing that happens, cannot a host of persons be said to have colluded?

Let us return to the question of why dreams may show us our shadow side. We can imagine our lives as having elements in which freedom is fully expressed and elements which are blocked or imprisoned. Energy may be trapped under the umbrella of negative feelings. If we push unacceptable feelings to the side and choose non-awareness, it may have the effect of creating a prison for us. So, a result of becoming aware of the shadow side is so that we can be free of the energy trapped by it.

There remains the question of how to express this shadow side and the moral dimension present. I suggest now that there are creative, non-harmful, symbolic ways to release or free the energy present here. We do not need to literally act out on the murderous impulse to release that energy. Perhaps the dream will even show us the path to such a release. In the case of the dream given here, it is going out from our "prison" and running free for a period which releases that energy.

7. Dreams Call us to Be More Aware, To Becoming & Doing

In this guideline we consider an overall orientation to the dream material that have considered. Our dreams are seeking to make us more aware. We become aware of a symbolic language that speaks about ourselves and others was an early guideline. Working backwards, the previous guideline was to become aware of the shadow dimension that our dreams are informing us about. Before that, we became aware of the archetypal dimension of reality that might encompass more fully our life history and trajectory. Importantly too, we found dreams deal about relationships, a critical dimension to our fulfilment and that of others. Then early on, we considered how dreams are a metaphor for a life situation. In short, dreams are a call to awareness. We come to know the fullness of reality more. The perspective gained, interestingly, is coming from our own depths, with possible spiritual inspiration, both of which we sense is coming from a truer place.

Dreams do not stop there. They do not simply make us more aware of what is current reality, but also help us envision reality yet to be. They involve opening the door of mystery. Things that are coming into consciousness and reality at this point in historical time may be articulated in a dream. Thus, dreams have a visionary quality to them.

Last night, 10/23/22, I had a brief dream, which I now relate:

> In my dream, I see an image of a smaller person. Inside, I see what looks like a drawn image of a double heart. I had been talking about symbolic things in a small group, and the topic of the double heart had come up. I say "Yes, I have dreamt that." Walking along with a person, he comments, "So, you've dreamt that too." Implying that I might have made that up.

This dream has definitely envisioned something more. We don't think of people as having two hearts. Thus, dreams convey an element of mystery. This mystery also enhances awareness. What does it mean? I recall a conversation I had yesterday with a music teacher from Texas, who loves both cats and dogs, but cats more. This person has both loves and, metaphorically, could be seen as having a "double heart." This phrase opens a door to expand my awareness of self and others, that persons should not be pigeonholed to one type, or one conception, which often diminishes that person in our eyes.

After this dream, a new title emerged from my writing and interaction with the dream world, one that featured not only meaning but also beauty and mystery. Meaning has been a focus in much of the guidelines already presented. Just now, I have touched upon the mystery of dreams as envisioning something more. Last, the new title brings up something I have not yet spoken about directly. Dreams have a beauty to them. Dreams are interesting and intriguing to us because of their story-telling capacity, their tight construction, and their fabulous imagery. They are an art form, employing a double power, an integration between narrative and novel imagery, which has deep symbolic resonance. Interestingly too, the dream I had last night has worked to expand my awareness about dreams, as if instructing me. It is awareness I had not yet directly articulated from my study or reflection to date.

Dreams, we sense, also call us to "becoming. The self can be seen as a process of becoming or unfolding. In this view we are not set in one mold, but rather we can grow and go through significant change. Our self can be seen as always growing and expanding in the dimension of love.

Last, dreams often involve a call to do something more. The dream just cited seems to not so much call for a specific direct action, but a more open frame of mind, leading me to look for the complexity in myself and others. When we become more aware and our self is becoming, we are led to take new actions. I will elaborate this concept more in the section on tools of dream listening or interpretation. For now, we suggest that dreams spill over into doing, meaning that dream awareness helps to create our ongoing reality.

In short, our dreams present a challenge and an expansion to our awareness, our becoming and our doing.

Part II
SEVEN TOOLS TO INTERPRET DREAMS

1. Write Down the Dream

Perhaps the most basic technique for remembering dreams is to write them down. Dreams come from a subtle space whose connection to this reality is fragile. It reminds me of Native American dream catchers, webbed constructions which seek to help catch fleeting dreams. When you wake and remember the dream, you can try to rehearse it in your mind so you can better remember it later, but the best thing to do is to try to immediately write it down.

If you remember one important image in a dream, you are more likely to remember the rest of the dream. The leading image serves as a type of key from which the rest of the imagery may flood. So, even if you jot down a few notes and go back to sleep, the full dream may await you when you get up. Even the smallest phrase you remember from a dream has significance. The fact you remember that part of the dream reveals something. Also, a fragment remembered is a signal that a fuller dream may await.

Let me give an example of a dream dated on a Sunday, 6/12/22.

> In my dream, I have a house jutting over the ocean with deep waters below. I realize that the house could fall into the waters when I am sleeping. Then I become aware that I'm in a different part of the house, and I'm sleeping under solid ground by the shore.

The initial part of the dream remembered is a house hanging over dangerous waters. That part likely stuck in my mind because it registered a state of alarm. The dream was short, and there may well have been more scenes. But I remembered enough to write down a vignette. In this case the dream message was a reassuring one. Even though I may feel like "my house" is in danger of falling into the waters, I'm actually grounded and safe.

In another dream last night (10/25/22), I wake and do not remember my dream right away. There's a short period of silence, a couple minutes of so, and I wonder if the dream "matrix" will release any image. Then it comes, a scene of me walking along a causeway along waters that are partially flooded and the water appears to be rising. Which way do I go, back from where I came or ahead to structures that look more interesting? An elaborate sequence of events unfolds from here, but the dream memory started from that precarious causeway. I got up and jotted a few notes, then typed up the full dream later.

Having a dream journal, or set folder on your computer, to house and date your dreams, is important. You are telling yourself that dreams are significant and need integration into your life. You will find that creating a record amplifies meaning gained from having a body of dreams.

The deeper issue is remembering the dream. Some people report they don't dream. However, we know we all have the biological correlates to the dream state, notably REM sleep, suggesting that we all dream. The question then becomes why do some people remember them and some not? We must assume the answer is partly cultural and partly individual orientation to the dream/symbolic realm.

Perhaps we need to ask and become more open to receive dreams. In ancient times there were temple spaces for you to incubate a dream, to receive a message from that realm. Likewise, in Indigenous North America, the vision quest to a remote place sought a vision experience which could include dream visions. We may consciously ask for dream messages, and we may unconsciously ask. Our deeper being may need a message and be open to one, allowing the dream to come.

From where do dreams come? From what world are they retrieved? Two broad theories are possible. Either our minds produce them or we pick them up as inspiration from outside of our mind. Maybe there is an interaction between the two, where the dream vision is received from outside but is also modified by our mind, making it more individual to us.

Perhaps I stray from the theme of this section. But writing the dream down honors the dream. Whatever its source may be, the dream world invites our respect, which then makes it more likely it will offer its gifts.

Remembering and writing is a basic step in listening and interpreting your dreams. Writing insures we remember. The word re-member invites us to consider that we are integrating a fragmented or dismembered part of ourselves. We are bringing to consciousness and the actions of our life, an awareness from the dream dimension. I would dare to say that our life course will more likely stay on track with such attention. Remember your dreams and write down the ones that speak to you.

2. Make Daily/Immediate Associations to the Dream

As you listen to your dream and write it down, associations will surface. These can be noted mentally or in writing. The key is to find out what domain or area of your life the dream is referring. Does it have to do with some situation at work, a particular relationship, or some possible future direction in an area of your life you are considering? Some dreams, as we've already indicated, can be more general or archetypal, having a broader meaning. It may be offering spiritual insight or understanding of the general trajectory of your life.

In the first dream offered as an example, in my effort to get "home," I need to pass through some dangerous neighborhoods. That is a reality of Baltimore, where I have lived and worked in neighborhoods which are dangerous, although my experience is that much beauty is present there. Recently I have attended a couple of urban farming events, showcasing abandoned lots converted into rich gardens. The dream shifts to a situation that refers to my work, from which I retired, so there is a host of feelings and experiences to that as well. These are associations that can draw upon our past and recent experiences. Dreams do not operate in a vacuum, but create a story using the elements of your life.

A dream may touch upon a current conflict. Here, knowing the specific details of the dream may clue you to the specific situation being addressed. Thus, you meet a person in the dream. Who is that person? Do you know them or not? What is their appearance? Details are critical in giving us clues and we are like detectives, sleuthing a meaning from the dream scene.

Sometimes a particular dream is not obvious as to its specific situation. Looking through my archive, I present this dream, dated 10/1/17.

I'm in an apartment I used to rent on North Avenue, a poor stretch of town in the middle of the city. I get a call from the landlady, with whom I haven't spoken in years. We recognize each other's voice. I say things are fine and hint only indirectly of work that needs to be done. In fact, there are wide openings to the outside, a second floor opening as a large as a door.

An association is present, as this dream recalls a past place where I lived. This neighborhood was in a relatively high crime area, which I left several years ago. But in the dream, I am there in the present. A lot of unfinished work at this house leaves it with wide openings. Does this refer to my artistic work that is unfinished? Does it refer to my general openness and/or feeling of vulnerability to others? Dreams often employ buildings or structures in various states, which can reflect the self. Perhaps the second-floor opening, as it is a higher floor, represents a posture of spiritual openness.

The theme of doors unlocked, and spaces in which anyone could enter and steal things have recurred from time to time in my dreams. My associations here don't appear to offer a clue to a specific situation, but the dream appears to be more about my general orientation, my sense of boundaries, permeability, and exposure to the world.

All in all, an early first step with dreams is to recognize any associations that come to mind. Your flow of everyday consciousness in relation to the dream imagery is connecting the two worlds. As you start to bridge this gap, an essential element of listening and dream interpretation has begun.

Perhaps the second-floor opening, as it is a higher floor, represents a posture of spiritual openness.

3. Be Attentive to the Phenomenology of Dreams

Phenomenology is a long, fancy word, which essentially means the basics of what appears and what happens in your dreams. That is, what type of persons do you encounter, in what settings, and what actions take place in your dream? Are the persons family, friends, or strangers? Are the settings nature oriented or more industrial city settings? Perhaps there is a combination of both, with one more frequent than the other. What is the basic action in the dream? Are you traveling, observing, hunting for something, or running from something? When you have interactions, are you fighting with the other or working together, or observing? Lately, I have had dreams about trying to get home, and having to pass through difficult territory to get there.

Let me give a couple examples of a looking at phenomenon. The first dream is dated 12/2/2018.

> I'm sliding down with another person into a church area, to the edge of several foot drop to another level. The priest asks us to move from the edge and be careful. Then I'm over the drop and racing with a strip of yellow glittery fabric furling with me. I wonder what its purpose is.

This dream calls to mind the settings of churches which periodically appear in my dreams. I'm with a stranger and a priest, who is not specific. There is movement in the dream: the first is a drop for which one must be careful. The appearance of edges and drop-offs is a theme in my work, and points to risks as we make adjustments in the vertical dimension. There is also a horizontal dimension of movement, where I'm racing with a yellow fabric furling behind me. The appearance of beauty through artistic work with a sense of flourish is also a theme in my dreams.

The advantage in occasionally looking at your dreams in this manner is that you peer into the structure of your psyche and see what archetypes are active. Further, you can compare the themes and see how they develop or express differently over time. Phenomenology also invites us to consider the frequency of a theme. Has it just appeared one time, or is it a recurring theme? In doing this exercise, I came to a greater awareness of the patterns in my dreams.

In a second dream dated 7/15/2018

> I'm passing a wall as a huge sea wave comes crashing over the barrier. It skids me deep into the land, zinging me along. I call out to my son, for I can't get to him. He answers from a distance that he's all right. I wonder how I was able to keep my balance.

This dream involves a setting by the sea, a common theme, partly due to my childhood homes near a bay and the Gulf of Mexico. Being encompassed by waves is also a recurring theme, which may represent forces beyond our control. Here again, I am by an "edge," just as the house that was over the ocean in the previous dream, and in both a safety concern arises. In this dream, I am concerned about the safety of my son, which also recurs occasionally.

The theme of approaching edges and keeping one's balance gives me pause for reflection. When am I close to an edge in a situation in which I have to decide what to do? How can I make a choice that will better ensure I keep my balance?

Let us consider another dream, dated 1/20/2022 on a Thursday.

> In my dream I'm trying to get back to a location in a town where I grew up in childhood, like Florida or Alabama, but the place is uncertain, like a vacation spot. I pass by a large fountain area, which I didn't know was there. It has huge, beautiful sea horses, with rainbow colors floating and moving

in the air. I don't have my camera, but I'm not so upset that I don't. But I need to remember the location so I can get back there.

Later on, I meet up with friends, and I kid about the place with the tree being in the way. They laugh, for it's not really in the way, but a spot you can leisurely enjoy if you are passing by.

The dream is focused on an unexpected image of beauty, sea horses flying in the air. Dreams offer images of beauty at times, creating a sense of wonder and mystery. In this case the image of beauty is accompanied by the mystery of union of opposites, as sea animals are flying in air.

We might ask why do dreams present beauty, and a beauty which is also inexplicable and intriguing? In terms of phenomenology, we may say that beauty is built into the fabric of the universe. I wonder if beauty is a call to wonder, creating a sense of mystery that there is to something more behind the beauty. Perhaps beauty is the universe's invitation to seeing something as not in the way, as I thought about the tree in the dream, but as something to leisurely enjoy.

Let us consider another dream, going back a few years, dated 9/24/2016, on a Saturday.

Last night I had a rich dream about seeing sea life at the inlet of a bay, Gardiner's beach, where I grew up as a child. Three huge colorful turtles that look like they have crab undersides swim in plain view. A yellow bat lies still in the water with its eyes open. The whole beach is full of people.

I want to take pictures, but my camera is wet, and I find it's partly filled with water. It takes a while to empty the water out, and once I do, I see the underside looks rusted. The camera is ready to shoot, but the tide has changed and the whole beach is empty of animals and people.

The dream presents a beautiful image of nature, which has intriguing elements. Turtles have hybrid, crab-like elements. A bat, which is not a water creature or one of the day, is underwater with eyes wide open. This image of nature's beauty again makes use of a union of opposites, which makes for an aura of mystery. I note that the phenomenon of rich life underwater, a recurring theme in my dreams, may be a symbol of my own unconscious fertility.

Something else is useful to note, which dreams often possess in terms of their structure. They make use of foils, or two contrasting images, so that they each stand out more. In this last dream, we have a beautiful mysterious nature scene. Contrasted with that is my attempt to record that beauty with a camera that is water-logged and rusted. By the time I am ready to use my device, this beauty of nature is gone. A scene filled with life and people is contrasted with an empty beach. This contrast creates a type of challenge and raises questions. Am I missing beauty and people in my effort to record it? In the dream six years later, with the floating sea horses, I am not so bothered by not having my camera, suggesting progress.

The phenomenology of our dreams invites us to a deeper analysis of ourselves, our patterns of behavior, our awareness of beauty, and our sense of mystery. Looking at the broad patterns and types of images presented in our dreams invites us to reflect on our selves and our life. With this greater awareness, we put ourselves more surely on the path to living the fuller life.

4. Sum Up the Dream in a Sentence

Dreams can be complicated and involved, like the first dream presented in this work. There may be several vignettes that follow a story line, and there may even be what appears to be a second dream with no obvious relation to the first. A helpful synthetic tool, particularly when faced with a longer dream, is to sum the dream up in a sentence. Identifying the essential action that describes what basically happens is a significant step in listening and interpreting the dream. You could go so far as to say that if you do this, you have captured the meaning of the dream.

For example, in the first dream cited, I faced dangerous neighborhoods, workplace demands, and a canal with deep waters. The action in the dream could be summed by saying. *As I try to get home, I face different barriers.* In this framing we see that identifying the meaning of "home" is important to the dream's interpretation. The several barriers presented invite a consideration of factors in my life that are hindering me and which invite me to focus on a lot of detail. But the single sentence invites the question, "What is home?" We all know what home is or is supposed to be. A place of love, emotional safety, and a domain where you exercise some control. Loved ones may live in your home and you invite friends and loved ones to visit. Sometimes we are on a quest which makes us feel far from home and creates a longing to return to home. There is also the notion of our final home and whether our being comes into eternity. I do not know come into any definitive interpretation. But we can see the device of summing a dream to a sentence invites further reflection, such as the book title suggests: the meaning of home, and beauty of home, and its mystery.

Let us provide a second example written on a Sunday morning, dated 8/19/18.

In my dream I'm running from soldiers down my childhood street, Jones Valley Street in Alabama. I tire them out, but I need to find a place to rest before other pursuers find me. I go down into a nearby culvert along Four Mile Post to travel hidden. This may be the wrong direction to go, for it's away from a psychiatrist friend I know in the neighborhood. I come across a young man who is suffering from a mental condition, and he's saying "Navaho, Navaho." My psychiatrist friend suddenly shows up in a convertible, riding atop the culvert. He can understand the language of the person in need and jokes about the need for wider education. Then part of the car, where the driver is, falls into the ditch. I'm having a conversation with the people inside the car, then remember my friend is trapped below. I call 911. My psychiatrist friend says he's OK and is glad that I called.

The dream has a lot of detail, some of which is not obvious as to how to interpret. Let me try to sum it up in a sentence. *In avoiding pursuers and trying to hide, I run into a person in need, and my psychiatrist friend, who (despite a crash) is able to help me.* It's a bit of a run-on, but in constructing this sentence, I sense how I am running from things and becoming distracted from helping others. What am I running from? What am I hiding from? The hidden subtext here is that this dream relates to my perceived life mission of telling the stories of those in psychological distress and reforming the mental health system. The barriers to the mission present themselves as the "soldiers," and my tendency to be private and hidden. Nonetheless, my life mission pursues me, as even in my place of hiding, a person with mental health needs presents himself. My knowledgeable psychiatrist friend appears as well, the one who once guided me through a symbolic world.

Here, the focus on the dream as a singular sentence helped me to enter the dream and take it a step further. In a sense the tool is a "trick" which invites us to focus and linger. We may not want to face a given dream's meaning, and pass over it cursorily. The dream I realize now also has elements of reassurance. I will, for example, find persons who awaken my sense of mission and who will help me in the task.

If all else fails in your dream work, sum up the dream in the sentence, and you will come into greater awareness.

5. Dreams Can Have More Than One Interpretation

Dreams are typically over-determined, meaning than can have more than one meaning. Generally, the rule in dream interpretation is to carry your understanding one step further than what you are now able to understand and act upon. You might revisit a dream later, even years later, and find further insights. Thus, it is best to have an open-ended approach. You will feel when something is the right interpretation and go with it, but that is for the particular time. All this being said, a dream may still have one main meaning with subsidiary ones.

Let us give an example of how to look at a dream in two different ways. In a dream, you can be in conflict with somebody, and even in a fight. You might relate this to being about a person or group you are having a current conflict with. However, the dream can also be viewed as the person representing a part of you and that you are fighting yourself. We more readily think of animals as representing aspects of ourselves, such as the dream of the three snakes and horse, related previously in the archetypal section. But people encountered in a dream could also be representing a dimension of ourselves.

Perhaps it is an irony that other persons we meet in the world, who are perceived as persons in themselves, might also reflect a dimension of ourselves. In psychology this may be called a projection, in which we overlay a view about a person which is more about ourselves. But perhaps, like in dreams when the other can also be a part of ourselves, there is more oneness with the world than we know.

Let us offer an example of a dream where we use a more expansive range of interpretation that includes this internalized dimension. In a dream dated 8/8/22:

> I am outside a presidential limousine, and they seem to be waiting for me to board. There are two spaces in the limo, one

in the front and one in the middle, and I take the one in the middle. I'm nearly squished between two people. The one on my right is an older woman who handles mental health issues. Earlier, I heard her refer to a compassionate care practice she had done a long time ago.

Then we are out of the limousine, and it turns out I know the President from his previous job. His name is Kelly. "I knew you before," and I tell him. "I am glad to meet you again. You're a person of general importance now, not that you weren't important before!" He acknowledges things, and I try to convey to him about my interest and the woman I met in the limo. It seems our eyes meet, and an understanding is achieved.

My dream relates to my sense of mission with the arena of mental health and my struggle to actualize and finish projects. The woman who had done compassionate care may refer to women I've interviewed in my book projects. The President in this case could represent leaders in the movement whom I've interviewed. In some cases, I interviewed them before they became more prominent in the advocacy field. This would then be a more external interpretation of persons in the dream, and how they might relate to people I've met in real life. I don't meet the President however, or drive around in his Limo, so the President and setting are more obviously symbolic. The President represents a person with strength in leadership and a strong leader with the power to execute things.

The other way to view the dream is to see the characters as dimensions of myself, with the limo as the self envelope. I chose not to be in front, closer to the President, but rather in the middle by the woman who has done compassionate care work. In my life, I have historically been more comfortable acquiring the vision, but not in exerting leadership to enact the vision. When I took the enneagram test, I realized these were opposites and that I needed to develop my weaker side, the one that exerts leadership in the world. Thus, the President could represent an aspect of myself, my leadership capacity. In this dream, the President and I have an interchange and we come to an understanding. The dream is encouraging, for it shows me that I am comfortable integrating this side of myself.

Looking at dream characters as representing others, complimented with the understanding that they can be a part of ourselves, illustrates the expansive or over-determined nature of the dream world. But there are other ways that dreams offer multiple meanings. As the book title suggests, dreams have a dimension of mystery that is open ended. We may not quite know what the dream means yet, though we may sense it. This is like people we meet, whom we might categorize and think we have captured who they are. Yet people grow and are an evolving book, and we have to work to catch up to who they really are and are currently becoming.

6. Warning and Reassuring Dreams

Whatever the source of dreams, our own deep intuition or messages from the universe, they are concerned with our well-being. This includes our physical survival. So, if such a danger is imminent, our dream world may well send us a warning. It's possible that a dream could warn you about the danger of your speeding which may cause an accident, or a friend in emotional need who is becoming suicidal. There is a long tradition of warning dreams having a saving effect in sacred traditions, such as Joseph's dream warning of seven years of coming famine in Egypt, to Joseph of Galilee being warned to protect his family from a murderous king.

The danger portrayed may be literal and/or symbolic, but it is a good idea to consider the literal danger first. Thus, if you are having dreams of your car breaking down, you might consider having it checked. In the past few years, I have had dreams of impending storms, such as water rising or tornadoes heading my way. I related this to the political, economic and pandemic turbulence of the times. In this case, the threat may not be literarily from hurricanes or tornadoes, as I don't live in that area of risk. Here is a dream on a Monday, dated February 1st, 2021.

I'm high in a skyscraper with others, and I see an unexpected form in the distance that I recognize as a tornado. It's in the midst of an urban setting. I rush to get out my phone camera and take photos as it passes to the left of us. The tornado takes unusual forms at points, losing the funnel shape and looking like brown-streaked lightning, frozen for moments in still frame, which I try to capture. Then it's ahead of us, but it starts to come circle back to us. "Hang on to something tight!" I yell to the others. If the tornado really comes this way, there is no way we will survive. Then it hits. the whole building shakes, and it falls. Somehow afterwards, I have consciousness amid the aftermath. I don't know how I survived.

This dream occurred about a month after the attack on the U.S. Capital. Along with this political upheaval and uncertainty, the country was in the middle of a serious pandemic, accompanied by a lot of economic uncertainty. This dream is warning that the destruction visited may yet circle back, and cause the whole building to fall. In the dream I am warning others of this danger.

This dream presents a danger that is communal, not a singular danger to me. Of course, people rarely heed such warnings, and believe messengers and messages are over-exaggerated. But I believe the dream world does not perform false flag operations, that it can fairly represent reality from a totality of clues, which we neglect at our own peril.

Out of my many tornado dreams, I choose another one dated almost four years earlier, on a Saturday, July 15, 2017.

> I am in a building with others, looking out a large glass window over the sea. Some trunk-like shredded structure is hung in the sky. Suddenly I realize what it is, and I shout out "Tornado!" and start to run. Then, from the center of the building, I slide down the funnel of the tornado. I land in the basement and continue to hurl through the basement underside, which opens to the outside street. I come back into the basement to a set of tables, to have food with others. You can still see the tornado in the distance. Someone asks if I am prophetic, if I can see the future, and I say no.

In this dream I am again warning people in a building about a tornado coming. I am early to recognize that the indistinct form in the distance will be a danger to us. Interestingly, the striking image presents of myself sliding down the funnel of the tornado. I take this now to mean that I feel and experience the heart of the danger and perhaps tame it. I'm hurled outside, but I come back to be with others. The danger has subsided for now, and someone asks if I am prophetic. I reject the designation which makes me the focus, rather than the danger at hand.

I imagine that there were many warning dreams from people in Ukraine, that their country was in danger, and that a "tornado" would soon whip through their land. I don't know if a warning dream prodded them, but grandparents on my father's side left that land decades ago to avoid the impending danger of WWI.

Warnings can be more personally directed, however, such as toward your own family. In a dream on a Sunday, 10/13/2019.

> It's raining hard, and water is rising to flood levels. My son is in a house on a hill and already the water is streaming over the house. It's too late to get him, and I'm swept out to sea. I wonder if I will go out to the ocean, and that it's my time to die. Then water current suddenly falls off, the streaming stops, and I'm slowly rotating in a small whirlpool.

> The scene suddenly changes, and I've come aboard to a party scene aboard a large boat. I see one of my brothers there, but I don't see my son, and I wonder if he will show. Somehow, I sense this is not real, and I make comments about that. A lady tries to stop me from speaking, even putting her hand over my mouth, so I won't awaken these people. I hear a reference to a person saying they are full of REM or enjoying the REM, a reference to dream sleep. I decide to run away, going out by way of the lower deck and into the water again.

> When I "wake" again, it seems it's more real this time. David, I find out, has escaped and gone to Michigan with his aunt. He should be safe then from the waters, I think.

This dream is concerned about dangers to my son and self from rising waters. Interestingly, I am again caught in a whirlpool which then sends me to a scene with other people. I am in a setting that is luxuriant and safe. But is that real? When I try to tell people that this party, with all its trappings, is not real, I am stopped from commenting. In this case, paradoxically in the context of this work, dreams and REM are referred to as preferred illusion to reality. Interestingly, my son yesterday was talking about the "matrix," how we are trapped or caught up in an illusory world, and how he has the challenge to be different. This dream, however, ends with a reassurance that my son is safe with an extended family member. Thus, the dream offers both warning and reassurance. There is risk of being disconnected from the reality of impending dangers, but there are safe places to be.

In sum, this section invites us to take seriously signs of warning that occur in dreams. They also ask us to be attentive to dreams showing us the path of survival, and one which offers reassurance.

7. Dreams as a Call to Action

One of the key insights of Ann Faraday's work is to consider dreams as a call to action. The proper resolution of a dream may well be to *do* something. This harmonizes with the early school of American philosophy, pragmatism, in which we are invited to dip our ideas into reality and test them. We can become aware all we want, but awareness will be limited if we don't act upon our ideas and see their results in reality. The action we are called to do may be very specific, such as to get in touch with a certain person. Or, the dream may throw out a possible new direction in life that will enrich you. We have already seen how a dream may try to keep us aligned or on track with a life mission.

The call to action is the last step in our work on dreams because it throws us into the world from which new experience will emerge. This then becomes the basis for reflection, and something more for dreams to build upon and inform us. Let me give two examples.

While I was writing this work, I had the following brief dream, dated 10/28/22. It was the first I came across in searching for an example.

> In my dream, I discover a new coffee shop that I wasn't aware of. I view the place, evaluating it. It has some individual seating, and a glass-paneled room with comfortable chairs set around a table. It looks like a place for group meetings or lectures, but it's empty now. There are youngish people about the shop, and music which is new and fitting the generation. Outside, I go toward a dark surfaced area which I first think is a lake and watch my step. But it is black pavement and I can cross it.

This dream relates to my desire to find some social connection in local coffee shops where I write. It also brings to mind newer bookstores, offering community events and greater social connection. This relates to the empty meeting room in the dream. The action for me may well be to visit such a café/bookstore and check out their activities. I know of a local owner with whom I should share about my publications personally, and perhaps do a presentation. After some random and unsuccessful attempts at just dropping by, I have avoided following up. Perhaps I have a fear of going there, as reflected in the dark surface, which brings up fears of a deep lake and drowning. This may relate to a fear of rejection of my work. However, in the dream, this barrier is something that I can easily cross over. The dream may not only be inviting me to visit a new bookstore/coffee shop, but reassuring me that this passage will be easier than I think.

After writing the above, I stopped my work and sent a detailed email to the bookstore owner I know, sharing about my recent projects and asking for a time to meet. I don't yet know the result of this, but the dream and writing this book have now motivated me to take an action. Doing such actions, I imagine, will empower your dream world. If the deep self knows that you are going to act upon its suggestions, then it will become stronger.

A second dream, which I had during my senior year in college, I now recall from memory, though I have written it down in journals. The dream, a mystical-like experience, had an influence on my life's direction.

> I have a strong feeling of dark wavy currents that hold an air of mystery; there's presence here I sense. Then I experience a bright yellow light in my mind and the thought of *God*. Suddenly, I fly up from my bed and embrace a body. I'm surprised that God has a body. In the last scene, I am in the streets of a city neighborhood. Some African Americans are cussing and yelling at me, and it feels dangerous.

The first part of the dream I interpreted to be about the Presences of God. The first is God as mystery and more unformed to our mind. The second is about the mental representation and name of God, which is experienced as a light in the head. The third is about the physicality embraced by God. Here, divinity is represented as not just something mysterious or a mental idea, but as having a concrete presence and body like us.

The last image did not seem to fit with the first three and took me a while to understand. I concluded that this, too, was about a presence of God. In this case God was found in poor urban areas which may seem hostile to us. This was quite far removed from me at the time, living at a college in the deep South. Yet when the choice came to me to move and attend graduate school, I selected (rather than Midwest Indiana) the urban coastal area of Baltimore, feeling I was being called to go there. Our lives become different, the composition of the whole social group around us, depending upon where we go.

I do not see dreams so much as giving us a directive that we blindly follow. Rather, if we are already feeling a call, we are given assurance this is the right path to take. It might, however, also be what tips us or gives us the needed motivational push to decide and act upon it.

In the previous example I notice too how the dream encompasses all three elements listed in this book's title. It offered meaning, showed beauty, and conveyed an air of mystery. Perhaps these are elements that excite us to action, that help make for and complete the drama of our lives.

Not all dreams are momentous and mystical, but they may become so at important junctures in our lives. Typically, however, our dreams are nudging us along to stay on the path that is truer to our deep self and keeps our integrity.

FINAL THOUGHTS AND EXAMPLES

We have taken a journey into the dream world, highlighting my own dreams as examples. Hopefully, you have gained a feel for how symbols operate and can become a second language to help guide your life. You have begun to sense the contours of my dream world, but for each person, there will be an individual quality based on each one's temperament and background. Part of the challenge in life is to find your own uniqueness and to maintain a harmony with a deep connection with all people. This tension of joining opposites is a challenge that the dream world does not shy from. It especially may seek to address those whom we feel are opposites and have difficulty approaching. Particularly at this juncture in his history, there is an extreme polarization occurring which is rivening society in half. With this in mind, I feel impelled to share this dream, dated December 29, 2016.

> I wake at 4:30 a.m., recalling a dream of strange rites in New Orleans. In a vignette, I gain firsthand knowledge of unusual events. Christ himself has returned with a friend who has also died and lived again. It seems I am limited in this one dimension and need to cross over to another. An unexpected ally appears, a brother-in- law, the husband of my departed sister. He's an unexpected choice, as we have different temperaments, and we are at opposite ends of the political spectrum. Still, I tell the ones in charge, who could release us to go on the journey together, that he is an effective person who can hit the ground running. I talk to him, sharing this unusual and important news, and that he needs to go with me.

The dream presents a mystical dimension, as can happen in my dreams. Here, the Christ Archetype appears, which in Jungian psychology represents the true Self. Interestingly, this dreams that the

Christ figure has a type of double who mirrors his story, and that the returned Christ does not operate alone. Having established this, the dream invites me to befriend this opposite person, making the case that this would make for an effective difference in the world. I can't say that I've risen to the challenge this dream presents, but I think it presents the challenge as there. And I dare say that many of us of late have similar dealings as this.

From this example, we see dreams are very concerned about relationships and the spiritual and political worlds. Importantly, too, they have a moral bias toward unity, and they call us to have effective action in the world.

We are called to pass on dream awareness to others. In my case, later in life than most, I had an only child with whom I have shared my dreams and asked about his. This has led to his remembering and sharing dreams with me. Thus, one morning I was not so surprised for him to tell this dream to me a few months ago in the summer.

> In his dream there are three mansions, and our family is hosting guests in one of them, some 40 persons. A next-door neighbor, who is a bearded and stocky, is unfriendly and has a huge dog. It's a killer dog with piercing blue eyes and scars. A friend of my son had taken something, like a flower, from this person's garden, and is at risk of retaliation. To help resolve this, I go with a person who carries a gun to meet this person. The problem was handled, but I died and didn't come back.

> The scene shifts, and my son sees me rising from a lake surrounded by bright light. I'm not actually seen, but I am raised by a divine beast that looks like an elephant.

Here my son senses the polarized world and that it could have the consequence of causing the death of someone close to him. However, the dream also shows that despite death dealing forces, there is a force of divinity in the world that can bring return and victory. Thus, the dream serves as both a warning and a reassurance.

The work posed by dreams is challenging, and we are not left with easy solutions. But if we learn to listen to dreams, we will find meaning, beauty and mystery. This will enrich our lives and invite us to make for a better world. When all is said and done, isn't that what we want, the world to be a better place because we have lived?

You have, I suspect from your interest in dreams, already begun this journey and are on the path.

Don't miss out!

Visit the website below and you can sign up to receive emails whenever Michael A. Susko publishes a new book. There's no charge and no obligation.

https://books2read.com/r/B-A-GJLJ-CNBCC

BOOKS2READ

Connecting independent readers to independent writers.

Did you love *The Meaning, Beauty & Mystery of Dreams: Seven Guidelines and Seven Tools for Listening*? Then you should read *Aging and Renewal: Living the Full Life*[1] by Michael A. Susko!

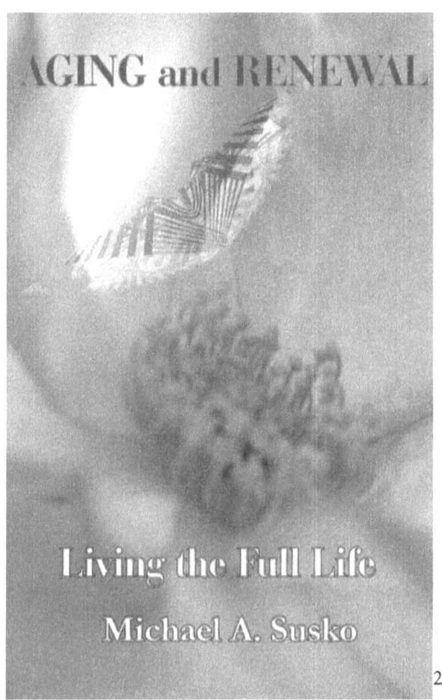

[2]

This book offers a vision of renewal as one encounters the novel obstacles of later life. Issues such as caring for the body are addressed, including the paradox of how a prior solution can become the problem. The basic triad of our biological-psychological reality is also focused upon: how we need to tend to consciousness, mobility, and the social dimension throughout our life. Read this work to gain needful insights and a vision which will help you to live a full life.

Read more at https://www.allroneofus.com/.

---

1. https://books2read.com/u/mlXE8W

2. https://books2read.com/u/mlXE8W

Also by Michael A. Susko

A Couple Through Time
Down Below and the Archon's Castle
Up Above and the Runaway
Across the Gulf and Journey Into Un-Time
On the Bay and a Child Found
In the Wild and Do One Wild Thing
On the Mountain and Two Are Missing
To the Beginning and Journey Through Here

Archetypal Worlds
Alwon in Another World: An Archetypal Voyage
Line On the Wall
The Alien's Gift
The Gold People
Spider Woman and the Timeroc
Quill Ears & the Other Earth
Darkwood and Dual with the Shadow Side
Giant Under the Mountain

Early Humanity

Haikus and Photos: Presence at Penn Bluff
Haikus & Photos: Mystery Form at Penn Bluff
Haikus and Photos: Essences at Penn Bluff
Haikus and Photos: World Archetypes at Penn Bluff

The Dreaming Series
Sleek Back
Streak and Cave Bear Dreaming
Moby and Marsupial Mole Dreaming

The Dream World Trilogy
Delphi, the Time Thief, and the Dream World
Detinna and the Cave God
The Resistance & the Empire

Transformational Stories
Caseness and Narrative: Contrasting Approaches to People
Psychiatrically Labelled
Transformative Experiences, Psychiatric Research, and Informed
Consent
Transformational Stories: Voices for True Healing in Mental Health

Writings from Street People
Street Images
Street Images II

Standalone
The Little People & the Time-Rider
Animal Spell: A Gospel Story With a Transformational Twist
Ten Pulses of Evolution & the Surprising Nature of Evolutionary Time
Up Above and Down Below
Life's Dynamic Vulnerability: A Paradigm Shift in Biology
Alien Ally
The Generation of LIfe: Imagery, Ritual and Experiences in Deep Caves
Twelve Suspects
2084: Clash of the Cults
Bats in the Future
Guard of the Dead and Other Gospel Stories
The Imagination Being
Ten Traits of Empire that Every Person Should Know
Aging and Renewal: Living the Full Life
The Meaning, Beauty & Mystery of Dreams: Seven Guidelines and
Seven Tools for Listening
A Rosetta Key for History: The Generational Pattern of Time

Watch for more at https://www.allroneofus.com/.

About the Author

The author, who has an advanced degree in Counseling Psychology has led groups on dream interpretation. Throughout his life, he has worked on his dreams which has led him to identify several useful guidelines and tools. The author also has a son, who has been asked about his dreams and which has opened up a door of meaning for him.

Read more at https://www.allroneofus.com/.

About the Publisher

AllrOneofUs Publishing seeks out work which will make a novel and qualitative addition to the world literature, and one that will last across generations. Many of these persons are in the later part of their life and have made exemplary contributions which are unrecognized. To cite a few examples, we recommend Rich Mullin's *Ethics and the Full-breasted Richness of Life,* John Susko's *Flowers of the Night: Musings from a Sentimental Son,* and Dr. Curtis Adams' *Psychosis and the Humpty Dumpty Story.*